do SEALS* ever . . . ?

*Sea Lions, Walruses, and Manatees

Fran Hodgkins

Illustrated by
Marjorie Leggitt

Camden, Maine
Guilford, Connecticut

Down East Books

An imprint of Globe Pequot

Distributed by NATIONAL BOOK NETWORK

Text copyright © 2017 by Fran Hodgkins
Illustration copyright © 2017 by Marjorie Leggitt

Book design by Amanda Wilson

This page, top, and page 32 © iStock.com/ujord; this page, bottom, page 7 bottom, page 15 © iStock.com/wrangel; page 5, top © iStock.com/lrosebrugh, bottom © iStock.com/Aneese; page 6 © Alex Mustard/NPL/Minden Pictures; page 7, top © Richard Robinson/NPL/Minden Pictures; page 9 © iStock.com/stephankerkhofs; page 10, clockwise from top left © iStock.com/mthaler, © iStock.com/ValerieVS, © iStock.com/lluecke, © Heike Odermatt/Minden Pictures; page 12 © iStock.com/bashta; page 13 © iStock.com/passion4nature; page 14 © iStock.com/pilipenkoD; page 16 © iStock.com/USO; page 18 © Steven Kazlowski/NPL/Minden Pictures; page 19, top © iStock.com/Zanskar, bottom, © iStock.com/TersinaShieh; page 20 © iStock.com/maiakphotography; page 22 © iStock.com/roclwyr; page 23 © iStock.com/BURDE-Photography; page 24 © iStock.com/atese; page 25 © iStock.com/ShinOkamoto; page 26 © iStock.com/MakingSauce; page 27 © iStock.com/Andrea Izzotti; page 28 © iStock.com/Naturalpix; page 29 © iStock.com/Nalu Photo; page 30 © iStock.com/halbrindley; page 31 © Doug Perrine/NPL/Minden Pictures

British Library Cataloguing in Publication Information available

Library of Congress Cataloging-in-Publication Data available

ISBN 978-1-60893-467-6 (hardcover)
ISBN 978-1-60893-468-3 (e-book)

∞ The paper used in this publication meets the minimum requirements of American National Standard for Information Sciences—Permanence of Paper for Printed Library Materials, ANSI/NISO Z39.48-1992.

Printed in the United States of America

SEAL
(Pinneped)

MANATEE
(Siren)

Introducing . . .
THE PINNIPEDS AND THE SIRENS!

When you think of sea mammals, you probably think of whales and dolphins. But there are other sea mammals. They are the pinnipeds and the sirens.

Pinniped (pin-ee-ped) is the name scientists use for seals, sea lions, and walruses. The name means "fin-feet." **Sirens** include the manatees, the dugong, and the extinct Steller's sea cow.

We'll talk a lot about pinnipeds and sirens. To make things easier, sometimes we'll call the pinnipeds "the seals" and the sirens "the manatees."

The siren was a mythological creature that sang to lure ships close to rocks.

Long ago, sailors used to mistake dugongs for mermaids. It seems that a lot of sailors needed glasses!

Do seals and manatees ever come out of the water?

Seals spend a lot of time at sea, but they come of out of the water to have their babies. Sometimes they will clamber out onto a beach or rocks to warm up or to sleep.

Manatees don't come out of the water. Like whales and dolphins, they are born and live their whole lives in the water.

Do seals and manatees have legs?

The legs of seals and manatees have changed over time into **flippers**. The seals, walruses, and sea lions have four flippers. Seals' flippers are weak on land, so they hitch themselves forward on land like huge caterpillars. Walruses and sea lions can rotate their hind flippers so they can waddle on land.

Manatees have only two flippers. Instead of hind flippers, manatees have a wide tail that propels them forward. And like whales, manatees cannot move on land at all.

Flippers are paddle-like fins.

How do seals and manatees swim?

Seals, sea lions, and walruses may look a lot alike, but their ways of swimming are very different.

Seals get most of their swimming power from their hind flippers. They can spread their flippers out wide, so they can push more water to swim quickly. They use their front flippers to steer.

Sea lions get their power from their front flippers and use their rear flippers to steer. They kind of fly through the water. Walruses swim in a similar way.

Manatees have rounded, flattened tails and swim very slowly.

What were seals' ancestors like?

The ancestors of seals were land animals. They had four legs. Seals' ancestors were a lot like dogs. In 2007, scientists found a "missing link" that connected pinnipeds to their doglike ancestors. It lived about 20 million years ago in lakes in Canada. It looked like an otter, only bigger. Scientists think that it could swim *and* walk, making it a strong hunter on land and in the water.

The scientist named this new seal ancestor *Puijila darwini*.

What about manatees' ancestors?

Manatees are most closely related to elephants. Their ancestors were probably hoofed mammals. They are the only aquatic mammals that are **herbivores**.

Herbivores only eat plants.

What is the difference between a seal and a sea lion?

Seals and sea lions are very different animals, and if you look closely, you'll see why.

Seals' flippers are covered with hair and have small nails or claws.

Sea lions' flippers are bare and don't have many claws, and their front flippers are very large.

Their hind flippers are also different. In seals, the hind flippers stick out backward. Sea lions can rotate their flippers, so they are under the **pelvis**. This lets the sea lion walk on all fours.

Seals tend to have several colors in their coats, such as black, gray, and white, which form spots.

Sea lions are usually one color, often dark brown.

Sometimes sea lions are called "eared seals." Sea lions have visible ears, but most seals don't.

The pelvis is a bowl-like bone that makes up your hips.

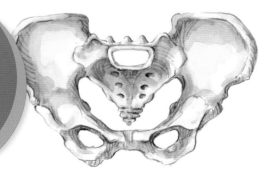

What is the difference between manatees and dugongs?

Manatees live in fresh water in the western hemisphere, mostly in Florida and the Caribbean.

Dugongs are sea mammals and live in the Indian Ocean and western Pacific. A dugong's tail looks like a dolphin's, while a manatee's tail is like a big flat paddle.

Male dugongs have short tusks, which are really their front teeth, that jut down from their upper jaw.

What do seals eat?

Most seals and sea lions eat fish and **crustaceans**. The leopard seal is an exception. It not only eats fish but also sea birds, including penguins. Sometimes leopard seals will eat other seals, too.

The leopard seal is the second most fearsome predator of the Southern Ocean, after the killer whale.

Crustaceans are hard-shelled sea animals such as lobsters and crabs.

What do manatees and dugongs eat?

Dugongs and manatees are plant eaters, grazing on seagrass and other water plants. They like to live in shallow warm water, where plants grow.

What's so special about a manatee's lips?

A manatee's lips aren't for kissing, they're for eating with! Scientists have found out that a manatee can control the way its lips move so well that it can use one side to eat a water flower and the other side to get rid of the parts it doesn't want.

Blubber is a thick layer of fat under seals' skin.

Do seals have fur?

Like other mammals, seals have hair. But because it's hard to swim if you're very furry, seals' coats are sleek and smooth. The water glides over their coats as they swim. But a thin coat isn't much help for keeping warm, especially in the cold ocean. So seals have an extra layer of insulation called **blubber**.

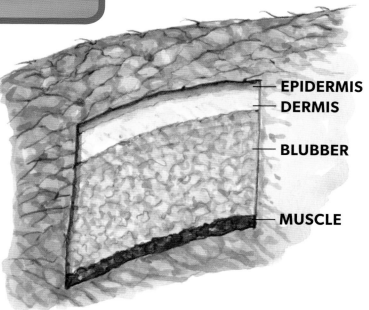

EPIDERMIS

DERMIS

BLUBBER

MUSCLE

Do manatees have hair?

Although they look hairless, manatees actually have fine hairs all over their bodies. The hairs aren't there to keep them warm but instead act like sensors, detecting movement.

Manatees often live in murky water, and any kind of movement could be a sign of danger. Thanks to these hairs, you can't sneak up on a manatee!

Walrus tusks can grow to four feet in length. What a tooth!

What do walruses use their tusks for?

All walruses, males and females, have tusks. They are made of solid ivory, just like an elephant's tusks. Walruses use their tusks for several things.

First, they use their tusks while they eat, but they don't use them to chew. A hungry walrus rakes the sea floor, sucking in clams and other mollusks, chewing and spitting out the shells.

Second, because walruses are really big, climbing onto an ice floe can be tough. So a walrus uses its tusks like a mountain climber uses an ice axe. They jab their tusks into the ice and use them to haul themselves up.

Third, they use their tusks to fight. Male walruses fight over the right to mate. Walruses also use their tusks to defend against predators like polar bears.

Do seals have teeth?

Seals do have teeth, and they can bite. Their front teeth are pointed, adapted for tearing food. The **molars** are made for cutting their food, and in many cases, look a lot like a dog's back teeth. The crabeater seal's teeth are very unusually shaped. They lock together in a way that lets the seal strain water out of its mouth while trapping **krill** inside.

Krill are like small shrimp.

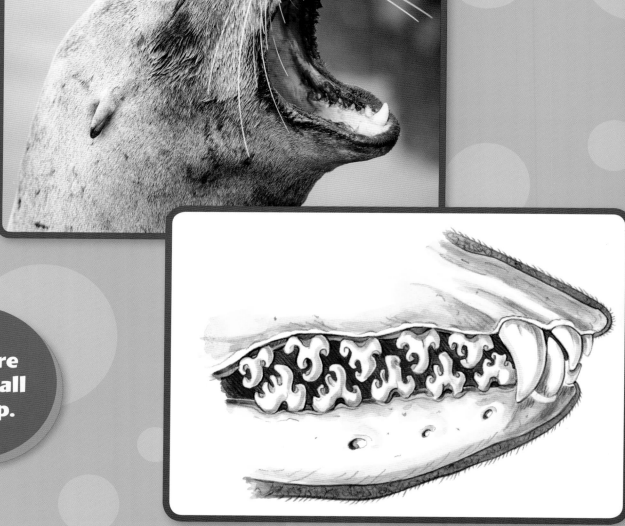

What's so unusual about manatees' teeth?

When a person loses a tooth, it doesn't grow back (unless it's a baby tooth). Manatees lose teeth all the time, because they wear out pretty quickly on the tough plants that these creatures eat. When a tooth falls out, the others behind it move forward, like they're on a conveyor belt. A new tooth grows in at the end of the row.

Manatees' teeth are called marching molars. The only other mammal with marching molars is the elephant.

Molars are the back teeth in an animal's mouth.

How big is the biggest seal?

The biggest seal is the elephant seal. The males of this species can grow to be 20 feet long and weigh up to 8,800 pounds.

Walruses are huge, too. They tip the scales at between 800 and 3,700 pounds.

How big do manatees get?

Manatees can grow to 13 feet long and weigh about 1,300 pounds.

How deep can seals dive?

Several seals are deep-diving experts. A female elephant seal was recorded diving more than 4,920 feet (1,500 meters) down. Weddell seals are also deepwater experts, diving as far as 2,000 feet. Elephant seals have been known to hold their breath for as long as two hours to make such deep dives. Seals can close their nostrils tightly to keep water out.

Can seals and manatees see well?

Seals' eyes are adapted to seeing under water. Seals' eyes have a layer called the **tapetum lucidium**. Cats and other animals that are active at night have this layer, too; it's kind of like night-vision goggles. This layer reflects light, so it bounces around in the eye.

Manatees don't see very well.

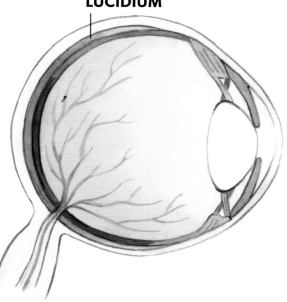

TAPETUM LUCIDIUM

A seal can see better under water than a human can.

Do seals and manatees burp and fart?

Indeed, they do! Scientists know that manatees develop a lot of gas because of their plant-based diet. In fact, they suspect that all that gas has caused a change in the manatee's skeleton. The manatee's rib cage is made of very dense and heavy bone. Scientists think that this heavy bone acts like a diver's weight belt, helping the manatee stay submerged despite all the, er, internal flotation that's going on.

How long do seals and manatees live?

The oldest manatee known to scientists was 65, but some manatees may live longer than that. They don't have many natural enemies because they are so big. In fact, in some places alligators and manatees live side by side. Their biggest threat is boats.

The oldest dugong we know of was 73.

Wild harbor seals live an average of 15 years. The record for a harbor seal is 47.6 years.

The record for a California sea lion is 35.7 years.

Andre was a famous harbor seal who lived part of each year in the wild and part of the year with the harbormaster of Rockport, Maine. He lived to 25 years of age—a very long life for a wild seal.

How do walruses sleep?

Walruses have evolved a special system that lets them sleep at sea. Inside their necks they have air pouches. When the walrus **inflates the pouches**, they hold the walrus upright in the water—just like a life jacket on a person. The walrus can catch some z's without needing to worry about keeping its head above water.

Seals and sea lions will come out of the water to sleep.

How do manatees sleep?

Unlike humans, who sleep for hours at a stretch, manatees catch naps. They may rest on the bottom or just below the surface of the water. On the bottom, they'll sleep for about 20 minutes, but they may come up for air without ever waking up completely.

If they doze at the surface, they'll take a breath every 3 or 4 minutes.

What should I do if I find a seal on the beach?

In the United States, seals and other marine mammals are protected by law. Only certain people can take care of them. If you see a seal on the beach, especially if it's a baby, you should leave it alone, because its mom is probably nearby. Watch the seal. If it's still there after 24 hours, call for help. Police and fire departments usually know how to contact marine mammal rescue experts.

As much as you may want to help, you need to wait for the experts. Trying to help can lead to you or the animal getting hurt—and nobody wants that!